W9-CNA-241

SERVING YOUR COUNTRY

THE UNITED STATES MARINE CORPS

by Michael Green

Content Consultant:
Captain Ben Tisa
United States Marine Corps (retired)

CAPSTONE
HIGH/LOW BOOKS
an imprint of Capstone Press

C A P S T O N E P R E S S

818 North Willow Street • Mankato, Minnesota 56001
http://www.capstone-press.com

Library of Congress Cataloging-in-Publication Data
Green, Michael, 1952-
    The United States Marine Corps/by Michael Green.
    p. cm. -- (Serving your country)
    Includes bibliographical references and index.
    Summary: An introduction to the history, function, weaponry, and future
of the United States Marine Corps.
    ISBN 1-56065-689-1
    1. United States. Marine Corps--Juvenile literature. [1. United States.
Marine Corps.] I. Title. II. Series.
VE23.G74 1998
359.9'6'0973--dc21
                                          97-31773
                                            CIP
                                            AC

Editorial credits
Editor, Timothy Larson; cover design and illustrations, James Franklin;
    photo research, Michelle L. Norstad
Photo/Illustration credits
Archive Photos/Charles Platiau, 16;
Michael Green, cover
National Archives, 10, 12
Unicorn Stock Photos/Aneal Vohra, 22; Robert W. Ginn, 30
United States Department of Defense, 4, 24, 26
United States Marine Corps, 8, 15, 18, 32, 47; Scott J. Olmstead, 20;
    Sergeant Mark D. Oliva, 28, 38; Mario P. Deangelis, 34; Jeff Viano, 36;
    R.L. Kugler, 41

Table of Contents

Chapter 1
The U.S. Marine Corps

The United States Marine Corps is one of the armed forces of the U.S. military. The Marine Corps is a specialized fighting force. Specialized means having the skills needed for particular jobs.

The Marine Corps specializes in amphibious warfare. Amphibious means able to work on land and in water. The Marine Corps' emblem shows its specialty. An emblem is a badge or sign. The Marine Corps emblem is an eagle sitting on a globe and an anchor.

The Marine Corps also specializes in amphibious landings. An amphibious landing is an attack on land by troops who come from ships. The Marine Corps also provides troops and equipment for air missions. A mission is a military task.

The U.S. Marine Corps specializes in amphibious warfare.

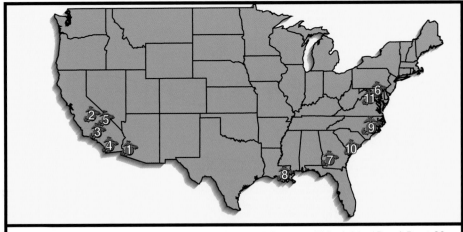

IMPORTANT MARINE CORPS BASES

1) Yuma Air Station, AZ
2) Barstow Logistics Base, CA
3) Camp Pendelton Base and Air Station, CA
4) San Diego Recruit Depot, CA
5) Twentynine Palms Air-Ground
   Combat Center, CA

6) Marine Barracks, D.C.
7) Albany Logistics Base, GA
8) Eighth Marine Corps, LA
9) Cherry Point Air Station, NC
   New River Air Station, NC
   Camp Lejune Marine Corps Division, NC

10) Parris Island Recruit Depot, SC
11) Marine Corps Headquarters, VA
    Quantico Marine Corps Base. VA

Peacetime

During peacetime, the Marine Corps keeps its personnel organized, trained, and equipped for war. Personnel are the people who work for the Marine Corps. It provides training for its military officers and enlisted personnel. Enlisted personnel are the people in the armed forces who are not officers. Their training includes learning military and career skills.

The Marine Corps protects U.S. military bases and embassies. An embassy is an official building in one country where representatives from another country work. The Marine Corps also provides troops for humanitarian and peace-keeping missions around the world. Humanitarian means something done for human good.

Amphibious Fighters

Marines are amphibious fighters and pilots. They are the first forces to fight during land battles. Marines also serve on warships. They help defend ships and fight during sea battles.

The Marine Corps works closely with the U.S. Navy. The Marine Corps does not have its own ships. Instead, marines serve on navy ships. During wartime, navy ships carry marines to battle sites. Navy ships often carry the Marine Corps' planes, too.

Marine Corps Structure

About 174,000 men and women serve in the Marine Corps today. Men serve in positions ranging from infantry personnel to officers. Infantry personnel are marines trained to fight on foot. Women serve in many of the same positions. But they cannot serve in all areas of active combat. Combat is fighting between militaries.

Most marines are active duty personnel. Active duty means full-time. They serve at bases in the United States and around the world. They work, train, and stay ready for combat. Other marines are reserves. Reserves are marines that stay ready for active duty. But they are not full-time marines.

The Marine Corps divides its troops into three large groups. Some active-duty marines serve in the Marine Forces Atlantic. Other active-duty marines serve in the Marine Forces Pacific. Reserves serve in the Marine Forces Reserve.

All the groups have combat, support, and command elements. Support means help. Some marines serve as infantry soldiers or pilots. Some help manage and aid missions. Other marines lead and control missions.

Marines in both forces must spend part of their tours of duty on navy ships. They also must serve part of their tours at Marine Corps bases. About 25 percent of marines serve on ships at one time. The other 75 percent serve at bases.

Women serve in many of the same positions as men.

Chapter 2
History

The United States Marine Corps became a separate branch of the U.S. military in 1951. But marines and the Marine Corps fought in many wars before 1951. The history of the Marine Corps starts with the Revolutionary War (1775-1783).

The Revolutionary War

In October 1775, the Continental Congress passed a law that created the Continental navy. The Continental Congress was the group of leaders that made laws for the American colonies. The Continental navy later became the U.S. Navy.

The Continental navy fought the British navy during the Revolutionary War. The British navy won many of the first battles. British ships had an advantage because they carried groups of marines. The British marines were sharpshooters. A sharpshooter is someone skilled at hitting small or distant targets. The British marines were also

The history of the Marine Corps starts with the Revolutionary War.

Marines helped General George Washington and his army stop a British attack on Philadelphia.

skilled at jumping onto and capturing enemy ships.

The Continental Congress created a force of American marines in November 1775. The American marines were part of the Continental navy. The marines helped the Continental navy win sea battles. American marines also protected the city of Philadelphia in late 1776. They helped

General George Washington and his army stop a British attack on the city.

The Marine Corps Act

The United States Congress broke up the American marine force after the Revolutionary War. Congress is the elected body of the U.S. government that makes laws. Congress believed there was no longer a need for marines.

By 1798, pirates and the British navy were causing problems for U.S. merchant ships. The pirates attacked ships carrying goods to and from the United States. The British navy also attacked U.S. merchant ships. The U.S. Navy could not fully protect the ships. Congress decided marines could help the U.S. Navy.

On July 11, 1798, Congress passed the Marine Corps Act. President Andrew Jackson signed the act and made it law. The Marine Corps Act established the Marine Corps. Marines served on the U.S. Navy's 26 warships. The marines strengthened the navy and helped it protect U.S. ships.

By 1812, the United States and Britain were again at war. The U.S. and British navies fought battles on the Atlantic Ocean and on the Great Lakes. The Marine Corps helped the U.S. Navy win many of the battles. They also helped defeat British landing forces at Baltimore and New Orleans.

The Civil War

The Civil War (1861-1865) was a difficult time for the Marine Corps. Many Southern states left the Union during the Civil War. These states formed the Confederate States of America.

More than half of the Marine Corps' officers left the Union military. They joined the Confederate States Marine Corps. Marines fought each other during the battles of the Civil War. Many marines died on both sides. The Union won the war in 1865.

World Wars

In 1917, the United States entered World War I (1914-1918). The United States helped France and Great Britain fight Germany and its allies. Allies are countries that work together.

Marines were among the first U.S. troops to fight. The marines fought as part of the U.S. Army's Second Infantry Division. A division is a large group of marines. The Germans called the Marines Devil Dogs. This was because the marines fought so hard.

During World War II, marines attacked islands that were under Japanese control.

The United states entered World War II (1939-1945) on December 7, 1941. On that date, the Japanese military attacked Pearl Harbor, Hawaii. The United States military fought battles in Europe and on the Pacific Ocean.

Marines made up a large part of the United States' fighting force in the Pacific. Their main job was to attack islands under Japanese control.

More than 90,000 marines fought during the Gulf War.

The marines won many battles on the islands. The islands included Guadalcanal, the Philippines, Iwo Jima, and Okinawa. Many of the island battles lasted several months. More than 23,000 marines died during the fighting.

The Korean and Vietnam Wars
In June 1950, North Korea attacked South Korea. This was the beginning of the Korean War (1950-1953). The U.S. government sent military forces to help its allies defend South Korea.

The first marines arrived in South Korea in August 1950. The marines attacked cities in North Korea. The Chinese army helped the North Koreans. Fighting continued for three years. Neither side clearly won. In 1953, North and South Korea agreed to stop fighting. More than 4,000 U.S. marines died during the war.

In 1965, the United States entered the Vietnam War (1954-1975). The Marine Corps provided some of the first U.S. troops in Vietnam.

The marines helped build military bases. They trained South Vietnamese soldiers. Until 1971, marines were a large part of the fighting force for the ground war. More than 13,000 marines died during the fighting.

The Gulf War

In August 1990, Iraq attacked Kuwait. The attack began the Gulf War (1991). The United States government helped Kuwait. Marines were among the U.S. troops that defended Kuwait.

More than 90,000 marines went to the Middle East. On February 24, 1991, the U.S. military began its ground attack. Two marine divisions fought their way through Iraq's defense lines. They attacked Iraq's forces in Kuwait. The Iraqi military surrendered four days later.

Chapter 3
Training and Ranks

People between 17 and 29 years old may join the Marine Corps. They must be in good health. Applicants must also be high school graduates. An applicant is someone who applies for a job or a program.

Most people who join the Marine Corps apply at recruiting offices. Marine recruiters make sure that applicants meet age, health, and education requirements. They also help applicants decide which jobs they could do in the Marine Corps. Applicants who meet all requirements enter the Marine Corps as enlisted personnel.

Officers enter the Marine Corps in different ways. Some officers enter the Marine Corps after graduating from military school. Other officers enter the Marine Corps after finishing college. They must first complete the Platoon Leaders

---

People between 17 and 29 years old who are in good health may join the Marine Corps.

Officer candidates learn important military skills during the Basic School Course.

Program. The program prepares them for Officer Candidate School. All Marine Corps officers must make it through Officer Candidate School and the Basic School.

New enlisted personnel and officers agree to serve at least one tour of duty. A tour of duty is a set amount of service time. The average tour of duty for enlisted personnel is three to four years. The average tour of duty for officers is four to six years. Many marines serve more than one tour of duty. Serving longer lets them increase their rank, responsibilities, and pay.

Officer Training

Civilians and enlisted personnel attend Officer Candidate School as officer candidates. A civilian is someone who is not in the military. An officer candidate is a military student.

Officer candidates take the Officer Candidate Course at the Officer Candidate School. The course teaches officer candidates the basic leadership skills. Officer candidates become officers when they successfully finish the course.

Officers then attend the Basic School. They take the Basic Officer Course at the school. This course is a series of training exercises that teach basic and advanced military skills.

Officers also attend training programs when they earn new ranks. New captains attend Amphibious Warfare School. Higher ranking officers attend Marine Command and Staff College and General Staff College. Sometimes officers also attend civilian colleges.

Basic and Specialist Training

The Marine Corps calls new enlisted personnel recruits. Recruits learn to be marines during basic

Drill instructors make recruits work hard during basic training.

training. Then they receive specialist training. Recruits learn how to perform their individual jobs during specialist training.

The Marine Corps has two basic training locations. One is the Marine Corps Recruit Depot at Parris Island, South Carolina. The other is the Marine Corps Recruit Depot at San Diego, California. The Marine Corps has the longest basic training program of all the armed forces. The program lasts 13 weeks. The Marine Corps also has the hardest basic training program.

During training, drill instructors make recruits work hard. Recruits wake up early and train until late in the day. They do exercises. They go on long runs and marches. Recruits learn about their rifles and practice using them.

Recruits receive specialist training after basic training. But they can also request other specialist training during their careers.

Ranks

There are nine enlisted ranks in the Marine Corps. Recruit is the lowest enlisted rank. Master gunnery sergeant and sergeant major are the highest. Enlisted personnel begin their careers in the Marine Corps as privates. They earn higher ranks as they serve and receive more training.

There are ten officer ranks in the Marine Corps. Second lieutenant is the lowest officer rank. General is the highest. New officers start as second lieutenants. Officers often earn higher ranks as they gain experience and training.

The Marine Corps gives enlisted personnel and officers pay raises when they earn new ranks. The Marine Corps also gives them small pay raises each year.

Chapter 4

Marine Corps Jobs

The Marine Corps has hundreds of different jobs for enlisted personnel and officers. Officers and enlisted personnel often work together in several job areas. A job area is a group of related jobs.

The main job areas in the Marine Corps include combat, aviation, legal, and technical areas. Aviation is the operation of aircraft. Each job area is important to the Marine Corps in peacetime and wartime.

Combat Area

Marines in the combat area are skilled fighters. They provide the fighting power necessary to fight battles. There are combat jobs in the infantry, the artillery, tank operation, and aviation support. During peacetime, marines in the combat area train and stay ready to fight. Combat marines

Marines serving in the combat area provide the fighting power necessary to fight battles.

Marines who serve in the legal area enforce military laws.

also make up the personnel for peace-keeping missions.

Marines in the infantry fight directly with enemies during ground combat. They make up a large part of landing forces. Marines in the artillery support the infantry. They fire cannons and missiles at enemy targets during battle. A missile is an explosive that can fly long distances.

Marines in tank operation drive and operate tanks. They provide moveable firepower for battles.

Aviation Area

Marines in the aviation area serve as pilots and support crews.

Pilots serving in the aviation area fly airplanes and helicopters. Pilots fly aircraft to provide support for ground forces during battle. They also fly aircraft to carry troops and equipment.

Marines who serve on support crews perform many jobs. They direct pilots on take offs and landings. They check flight equipment. Marines on support crews also maintain aircraft.

Legal Area

Marines in the legal job area enforce military laws. Enforce means to make sure laws are obeyed. They make sure that all marines receive fair legal treatment. They also work with marines who break military laws. Jobs in the legal area include military police officer, lawyer, and correction officer.

The military police are the Marine Corps' police officers. They help keep order at Marine

Marines who serve in the technical area set up and repair the Marine Corps' communication systems.

Corps bases. Sometimes they have to arrest marines who break the law. Marine lawyers and legal staff prosecute and defend marines who break military law. Prosecute means to take a person to court for committing a crime. Marines who do corrections work help run the Marine Corps' prisons.

Technical Area

The Marine Corps has many kinds of technicians. A technician is a person who sets up equipment and keeps it running. Technicians serve at bases, on ships, and on battlefields.

Communications technicians set up and repair the Marine Corps' communication systems. Communication is the sharing of ideas and information. Communications systems include telephones and radios.

Computer technicians set up and repair the Marine Corps' computer systems. The computers store important information about missions and daily operations. They hold the Marine Corps' records. Computers also help control the Marine Corps' aircraft, automobiles, and some weapons.

Other Job Areas

There are many other job areas in the Marine Corps. These areas include automobile repair, aircraft repair, construction, and engineering. Engineering is the science of planning and building machines and structures.

Chapter 5

Weapons and Equipment

The Marine Corps uses weapons and equipment to carry out its combat missions. The weapons and equipment help marines attack enemies and defend themselves.

The M-16A2 Rifle

Rifles are marines' most important weapons. Marines learn that their rifles are their best friends. This is because marines depend on their rifles to stay alive during combat.

The M-16A2 is the standard Marine Corps rifle. The M-16A2 is light. It weighs about eight pounds (3.6 kilograms). This makes it easy to carry and use. The rifle is also powerful. The M-16A2 can fire one round at a time or three-round bursts. A round is a bullet. The M-16A2 has a dependable range of 500 yards (457 meters).

The M-16A2 is the standard Marines Corps rifle.

Marines fire stinger missiles from shoulder launchers.

Machine Guns

Marines use many kinds of machine guns. A machine gun is a gun that fires many rounds rapidly. Machine guns are useful when marines need heavy firepower.

The Squad Automatic Weapon (SAW) is one of the Marines Corps' newest machine guns. The SAW is a hand-held machine gun. But it also has a bipod. A bipod is a two-legged stand. The SAW can fire up to 750 rounds per minute. It has a range of 1,094 yards (1,000 meters).

Howitzers and Missiles

Marines use different kinds of weapons to support the infantry during battle. These weapons are long-range weapons. They allow marines to attack distant enemy targets.

Howitzers are one kind of long-range weapon. A howitzer is a cannon that shoots explosive shells long distances. Marines tow large howitzers to battlefields with trucks. The M-198 is one of the Marine Corps' largest howitzers. The M-198 can shoot up to four shells per minute. It has a range up to 14 miles (22.5 kilometers).

Missiles are some of the Marine Corps' most powerful long-range weapons. Stingers are one kind of missile. Stingers are small missiles. Marines use them to shoot at low-flying planes and helicopters. Marines fire stingers from shoulder launchers. A launcher is a device that shoots some kinds of explosives. Stingers have a range of one to five miles (1.6 to 8 kilometers).

Armored Vehicles

Marines use armored vehicles in combat. An armored vehicle is an automobile or craft with a protective metal covering. Marines use armored vehicles to attack enemies and to carry troops and equipment.

Harriers can hover.

The Marine Corps uses tanks to attack enemies and support the infantry. M1A1 Abrams tanks are the Marine Corps' main battle tanks. Each tank has machine guns and a large, main gun. The main gun has a range of three miles (4.8 kilometers). Abrams tanks weigh nearly 68 tons (61 metric tons). But they can travel up to 42 miles (67.6 kilometers) per hour.

The Marine Corps uses Assault Amphibian Vehicles (AAVs) to carry troops from ships to the shore. AAVs can carry troops from the shore to sites further inland. Each AAV can carry 24 marines. AAVs travel up to 45 miles (72 kilometers) per hour on land. They travel up to 5 miles (8 kilometers) per hour on water. AAVs have machine guns.

Planes and Helicopters

The Marine Corps has its own small force of jet planes and helicopters. Some of the aircraft are attack aircraft. Others are transport aircraft. Transport aircraft carry supplies and personnel.

The Marine Corps' main attack jets are F/A-18 Hornets and AV-8B Harriers. Harriers can hover. Hover means to float above a surface. Hovering lets Harriers take off from and land in small areas. Both planes carry missiles and guns.

The KC-130 Hercules is the Marine Corps' main kind of transport plane. These large planes carry troops, equipment, and military vehicles. Some Hercules planes carry fuel. They can refuel other aircraft while in midair.

AH-1W Super Cobras are the Marine Corps' main kind of attack helicopter. These helicopters have missiles and guns. The Marine Corps uses Super Cobras to attack enemy targets on land.

SUPER COBRA

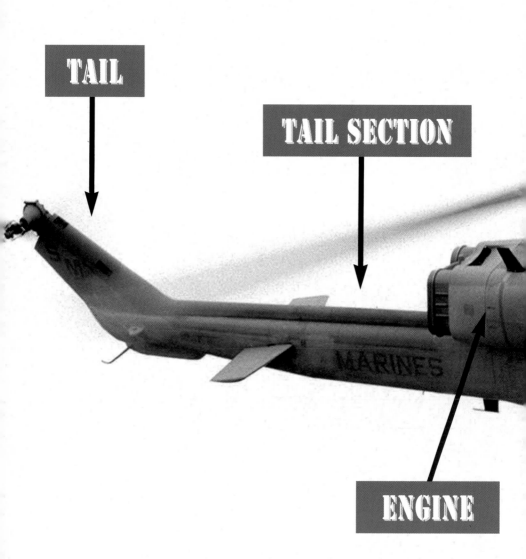

TAIL

TAIL SECTION

ENGINE

BLADES

COCKPIT

GUN

MISSILE RACKS

Chapter 6
The Future

Today, some U.S. leaders believe there is little chance of major wars. They also believe there is no need for a large U.S. military. Because of this, the U.S. government has cut some funding to the country's military.

The U.S. Marine Corps has become smaller because of these funding cuts. It has closed some of its bases and reduced the number of troops.

But the Marine Corps is still strong. It continues to defend the United States and help its allies. The Marine Corps has a new mission. It plans to build new equipment to help marines accomplish this mission.

The Marine Corps' Mission
The Marine Corps' mission is to help keep peace around the world. The Marine Corps and the U.S. Navy work together as expeditionary forces. Expeditionary forces patrol the world's oceans.

The Marine Corps' mission is to help keep peace around the world.

The expeditionary forces have two main goals. One goal is to stop conflicts from happening. Another goal is to end conflicts before they become large wars. So far, the presence of the expeditionary forces has prevented many conflicts.

New Equipment

Marines are depending on new equipment to compete with other militaries. The Marine Corps plans to use a new kind of fighter jet. It also has plans to develop and use a new kind of amphibious assault vehicle.

The Joint Strike Fighter (JSF) is the new kind of plane the Marine Corps wants to use. The JSF costs less money to manufacture than other fighters. But it is as effective as other jet fighters.

The JSF has many features the Marine Corps needs. It is faster and easier to steer than the Marine Corps' F/A-18 Hornets. The JSF can also hover in midair.

The Advanced Amphibious Assault Vehicle (Advanced AAV) is a new kind of amphibious assault vehicle. The Marine Corps wants to replace its older AAVs with Advanced AAVs.

One of the Marine Corps' goals is to end conflicts before they become large wars.

Advanced AAVs are slightly smaller than the older AAVs. They can carry 21 marines. But the Advanced AAVs are much faster. They can travel up to 50 miles (80.5 kilometers) per hour on land. Advanced AAVs can travel up to 45 miles (72 kilometers) per hour on water.

WORDS TO KNOW

allies (AL-eyes)—countries that work together

amphibious (am-FIB-ee-uhss)—able to work on land and in water

armored vehicle (AR-murd VEE-uh-kuhl)—an automobile or craft with a protective metal covering

aviation (ay-vee-AY-shun)—the operation of aircraft

combat (KOM-bat)—fighting between militaries

Congress (KON-gress)—the elected body of the U.S. government that makes laws

Continental Congress (KON-tuh-nen-tuhl KON-gress)—the group of leaders that made laws for the American colonies

division (di-VIZH-uhn)—a large group of marines

enlisted personnel (en-LISS-tuhd purss-uh-NEL)—the people in the armed forces who are not officers

howitzer (HOU-ut-sur)—a cannon that shoots explosive shells long distances

humanitarian (hyoo-man-uh-TER-ee-uhn)— something done for human good

launcher (LAWNCH-ur)—a device that shoots some kinds of explosives

missile (MISS-uhl)—an explosive that can fly long distances

prosecute (PROSS-uh-kyoot)—to take a person to court for committing a crime

recruiting office (ri-KROOT-ing OF-iss)—a place where people apply to join the military

reserves (ri-ZURVZ)—troops that stay ready for active duty but are not full-time marines

round (ROUND)—a bullet

sharpshooter (SHARP-shoo-tur)—someone skilled at hitting small or distant targets

specialized (SPESH-uh-lized)—having the skills needed for particular jobs

technician (tek-NISH-uhn)—a person who sets up equipment and keeps it running

tour of duty (TOOR UHV DOO-tee)—a set amount of service time

TO LEARN MORE

Green, Michael. *Amphibious Vehicles*. Mankato, Minn.: Capstone Press, 1997.

Green, Michael. *The United States Navy*. Mankato, Minn.: Capstone High/Low Books, 1998.

Hole, Dorothy. *The Marines and You*. New York: Crestwood House, 1993.

Rowan, N.R. *Women in the Marines*. Minneapolis: Lerner Publications, 1994.

Warner, J.F. *The U.S. Marine Corps*. Minneapolis: Lerner Publications, 1991.

USEFUL ADDRESSES

Marine Corps Air-Ground Museum
2014 Anderson Avenue
MCCDE
Quantico, VA 22134-5002

Marine Corps Historical Center
Building 58
Washington Navy Yard
Washington, DC 20374-5060

Marine Corps Division of Public Affairs
Headquarters Marine Corps
2 Navy Annex
(The Pentagon, Room SE-774)
Washington, DC 20380-1775

INTERNET SITES

MarineLINK
http://www.usmc.mil/

Semper Fi, Mac!
http://cpcug.org/user/gyrene/index.html#usmc

U.S. Navy: Welcome Aboard
http://www.navy.mil/

The U.S. Marine Corps continues to defend the United States and its allies.

INDEX